KATHY KI ER

A play with music abou l

by

Tom O'Brien

tomobrien2004@yahoo.co.uk

KATHY KIRBY: SINGER

A play in two acts

A shorter version called **KATHY KIRBY: ICON** was first performed at The Etcetera Theatre, 265 Camden High Street, London NWI 7BU as part of Camden Fringe Festival from 16th – 20th Aug 2012. Cast as follows; Anthony Cable, Martin Steven Carlton, Charles Davies, Victoria Farley, Roni Page. Musical Director Barry Potts. Directed by Tim Heath. Produced by David Donegan. (www.kathykirby.info)

Characters

KATHY KIRBY – blonde, 20s- late 50's

BERT AMBROSE manager/lover –50's-early 70'ss

MJ - Kathy's manager – mid 30s

LARAINE MCKAY - Kathy's lover – early 30's

FRED PYE Kathy's husband – 40's

SARAH – Kathy's niece – late 30's

ACT 1

Opening scene. The Eurovision Song Contest 1965. Kathy sings I BELONG.

VOICE: And now ladies and gentlemen, the 1965 Eurovision Song entry for Great Britain , Kathy Kirby.

KATHY:

I belong, I belong, I belong
Since half my life
My heart's been sleeping
For all this time
My love's been keeping

And now my heart has recovered
From past affairs that turned wrong
All my dreams are uncovered
I belong, I belong, I belong

At first I thought
Just one more lover
But then I found
Why he's like no other

And now my heart has recovered
From past affairs that turned wrong
All my dreams are uncovered
I belong, I belong, I belong

Too many hours slipped away
Too many loves came my way
But they only broke my heart in two
What it needs is someone just like you

At last you came
And from now on
The two of us
Will be as one

Yes now my heart has recovered
From past affairs that turned wrong

All my dreams are uncovered
I belong, I belong, I belong

Loud applause, blackout.

1980's. A seedy dressing room. Music in the background – the Bert Ambrose Band playing BYE BYE BLUES. After a little while the music fades.

A middle-aged KATHY KIRBY sits at a dressing table applying make-up. A teddy bear sits prominently in a chair nearby. (The teddy bear is called BENJY, is a big part of Kathy's life, and goes everywhere with her). She pours wine or gin into a glass and has a drink. She sings a few lines from I'LL CRY IF I WANT TO CRY

KATHY: It's my party, and I'll cry if I want to
Cry if I want to, cry if I want to
You would cry too if it happened to you.

She offers the teddy bear some drink.

KATHY: Would you like some, Benjy? Go on, have some with Mama. (she drinks) before my manager comes back. (laughs) Manager!

She looks around

KATHY: Where is this fucking place? MJ!

MJ, her manager, pokes his head in the doorway.

MJ: The Cockleshell Club.

KATHY: I slept all the way here.

MJ Well, chop, chop. Come on Kathy, get a grip.

KATHY: It's Miss Kirby to you.

MJ: Okay...Miss Kirby. Get your arse in gear, you're on stage in five minutes. (Exits)

KATHY: Come back here!

MJ returns.

KATHY: You're supposed to be managing my affairs, taking care of me. And where do I end up? This crappy dump.

MJ: Well, I did try the Palladium, but this 'dump' pays more. Look, it's better than sitting alone in your flat, toasting your shins on your lousy two-bar electric fire. Who knows where it might lead.

KATHY: To another crappy dump twenty miles down the road, that's where. Look at me MJ; I topped the bill at the bloody Palladium.

MJ: That was almost twenty years ago..

KATHY: Get me some decent bookings. That's not too much to ask. Bert would never ask me to lower myself like this. What will he say when he finds out?

MJ: Bert Ambrose is dead.

KATHY: I know that. I know that! It was ten years this very day.

MJ: (shamefaced) Oh. I'm sorry.

KATHY: I still miss him. Oh, I know people said he was too old for me, but what has age got to do with it? If you love someone, you just love him. How much older than me do you think he was?

MJ: I really don't know.

KATHY: Forty two years. He always said meeting me saved his career. "I was all washed up, ready for the knackers yard", he used to say, "and then you came along, gel". I was sixteen. That would have made him...fifty eight.

MJ: You want my opinion? I think he saw you coming.

We now hear the BERT AMBROSE band in the background playing a melody. There could be b/white images shown, or b/w film if available.

KATHY: Just listen, will you! The Ilford Palais, that's where it happened. Him and the band were playing there. And I remembered that it was Ambrose who gave Vera Lynn her first big break. She sang with the band for three or four years, and then she was made. And I was thinking "I can sing as well as Vera" so I just got up on stage and sang....

(sings) There'll be bluebirds over...

MJ: (sarcastic) I don't think I know that one.

KATHY: He signed me up straight away. He said I could be the next Vera Lynn. I told him I wanted to be the first Kathy Kirby.

MJ: That's all very interesting, but you're supposed to be on stage in the next few minutes.

KATHY: The next few minutes, the next few hours, what does it matter in the great scheme of things? Where are my Smarties?

MJ: Your...what?

Kathy finds a small pill box and takes a red pill out

Kathy: Who will care tomorrow?

Kathy washes down the pill with a drink

MJ: I will if you don't get on bloody stage now. Who's going to pay for this fiasco?

KATHY: I always pay my way. You won't be out of pocket, MJ, if that's what's bothering you. My bank account is healthy.

MJ: No it isn't. You've been broke for years.

KATHY: That's not true. Bert told me there was plenty there.

MJ: When did he tell you that? Jesus, Snap out of it will ya!

KATHY: He said....(she calls out) Tell him, Bert

MJ picks up the pill box and looks at it

MJ: How many of these have you taken? (Kathy shrugs) Jesus! Ambrose spent all your money, you stupid cow. Don't you remember? He's the reason you're in this state. Now, come on, time to sing for your supper.

KATHY: I'm not going on! You can't make me. I need another drink. (she helps herself) If only someone was here to guide me...Where's Bruce?

MJ: Bruce?

KATHY: Bruce Forsyth, who do you think! He was wonderful. We were wonderful together.

Kathy imagines Bruce. She sings SMILE as he dances with her

Smile, though your heart is aching
Smile, even though it's breaking
When there are clouds in the sky
You'll get by

KATHY: Do you remember our first meeting?

'Course you do! In the canteen at Decca recording studios. What was that song I was recording?

(She pushes him) Go on, you know!

(she sings the first line) Once I had a secret love...

You said I looked so...alone.

I was alone. And lonely. Bert was away on some business or other and I really didn't know anybody there. You bought me a coffee and made me laugh for the whole time you were there.

Make 'em laugh, that's my motto, you said.

It's certainly the way to a girl's heart. I've been laughing ever since.

We have a good time, don't we? Do you know that it's our anniversary this week?

Six months since we first met. We should celebrate...do something.

(pause) Maybe you should ask me to marry you...

pause

KATHY: But you did ask me, didn't you? You did. I'm not imagining it. I should have said yes...I would have said yes but for… but for your wife

And then you said ' Penny and me haven't been seeing eye to eye for quite a while now. I don't think our marriage is going to last much longer.'

(pause) And then you told me you were in love with me.

She comes back to reality

KATHY: I felt the same way about him. Then Ambrose found out and became terribly jealous. It nearly finished my career. I discovered that a Hollywood movie was offering me a three-picture deal. They thought I could become the British Doris Day. I desperately wanted to do it, but Ambrose would not to go through with it. He was turning down work for me because he thought I would leave him for Bruce.

MJ: Yes. Marvellous. Bert, Bruce...any more suitors I should know about? On second thoughts, we haven't got time for this...

KATY: Yes, now that you mention it. There was Tom...Tom Jones, Jimmy Saville...(she smiles) Benjy.

MJ: Benjy?

Kathy picks up the bear

KATHY: Yes. You're a lot more lovable than most humans I know, aren't you, Benjy? Do you know that his eyes twinkle when he likes somebody?

MJ: (looking at his watch). Let's go, you're late.

KATHY: That's a lady's prerogative.

MJ: It's not a bloody date! It's an audience out there – and they have paid good money to hear you.

KATHY: My fans are loyal – and they love me. And they will understand why I can't go on.

MJ: And why can't you?

KATHY: Because ...because this is not me. Look, this is somebody else in my body.

MJ: Oh, for Christ's sake!

KATHY: It's true. I don't recognise this person. (she looks in the mirror) Somebody has stolen my legs. All the girls on the street have Kathy Kirby legs. Have you noticed? My legs. I couldn't possibly go on stage like this. I'm not the real Kathy Kirby.

MJ: Who are you then?

KATHY: I don't know. I just feel it's not me who's standing here. She's just a stranger. (pause) I didn't get a wink of sleep last night. I am being held prisoner in my flat. I am being possessed by Bert. And others. And the Queen Mother is in me.

MJ: Well tell her to piss off.

KATHY: Why won't they leave me alone?

MJ: Oh Christ!! It's worse than I thought. (pause) Look, just pretend it's you. You always said you were a great actress, so go out there and prove it.

KATHY: I can't do that.

MJ: Who will know? – just you and me.

KATHY: Do you think it will work?

MJ: Of course it will. They won't be able to tell the difference.

KATHY: Well, if you are sure. Is it a big audience tonight?

MJ: A full house, darling.

Kathy takes a quick look

KATHY: They look like a bingo audience

MJ: That's because they are a bingo audience.

KATHY: I just hope they don't start waving their cards and shouting 'Housey, housey when I go on!

MJ: If they do it will be because they love you, darling.

KATHY: How do I look?

MJ: You look ravishing. Now, go out there and wow them.

Lights go down briefly then we see her in the spotlight. Loud applause and whistling. She sings SOMEONE TO WATCH OVER ME.

KATHY: There's a somebody I'm longin' to see
I hope that he, turns out to be
Someone who'll watch over me

I'm a little lamb who's lost in the wood
I know I could, always be good
To one who'll watch over me

Although he may not be the man some
Girls think of as handsome
To my heart he carries the key

Won't you tell him please to put on some speed
Follow my lead, oh, how I need
Someone to watch over me
Someone to watch over me

New scene 1980's

Kathy sits alone, eating a meal in her flat, drinking wine. She plays a record, then dances alone, watching herself in the long mirror. She appears to be in a trance (she is always like this after a performance, not quite with it) Unnoticed by her, Bert Ambrose appears from the 'ether'. He is a man in his early

sixties, immaculately dressed in a suit and tie, looking very suave, with an East End accent.

KATHY: Would the lady care to dance? Why did I bring you along, Mother? You embarrassed me as usual. You can't hold your drink, that's why. And the lighting! I had to follow the beam rather than the beam following me. (she twirls around) When Adam delved and Eve span/who was then the gentleman...

Ambrose has been watching her for some time.

BERT: What are you doing? Do you know that it's three a.m?

KATHY: Bert, Bert...oh Bert!

BERT: Ambrose, please. You know I don't like being called Bert.

KATHY: Yes, I've always known your preferences. But...I can call you what I like now...Bert.

Pause while Bert stares at her

BERT: And how was tonight's show?

KATHY: The band was out of tune, the pianist started in the wrong key, my voice was shaky, the audience were morons, and mother disgraced herself again – apart from that it was fine. And do you know where it was? Some godforsaken dump outside Newhaven.

BERT: Well, I hope you behaved in a professional manner. The way I taught you to.

KATHY: It **was** a long time ago.

BERT: You had a good teacher.

KATHY: You should have been there tonight.

BERT: You know that wasn't possible. I had others matters to attend to.

KATHY: Oh yes, baccarat, chemin de fer, blackjack. You always did like spending my money in style.

BERT: Is there any other way?

KATHY: Do you know how many managers I have had since you...departed?

BERT: None of them measured up?

KATHY: No. I'm just so fed up.

BERT: Oh, come on baby. What's there to be fed up about?

KATHY: Well, for a start you never take me anywhere.
BERT: We have to be careful, Kathy. There are some bad people out there, just waiting to drag a person's reputation through the mud. It's a game, with the press I mean. First they build you up and then they set about knocking you down. Have people been asking questions? About you and me?
KATHY; What kind of people?
BERT: Bloody reporters. Looking for something juicy to plaster all over their weekend rags. EXCLUSIVE – KATHY KIRBY AND TOM JONES. BIGGER EXCLUSIVE – KATHY KIRBY AND BERT AMBROSE. Don't tell them anything.
KATHY: I don't. You're my manager - that's all they know.
BERT: Good girl. That's the ticket. A shut mouth catches no flies. Besides, you don't have time to go out. What with all your TV appearances and live performances. (he looks around the room) And you live in this beautiful apartment in Mayfair – what more could a girl want?
KATHY: I'm lonely.
BERT: The whole world is lonely, darling.
KATHY: No! I mean I'm really lonely. I want someone - you - to put your arms around me, and tell me everything will be all right
BERT: I don't understand. You have a Mayfair home, beautiful clothes, a successful career, staff to wait on your every need...

We hear the strains of a song in the background briefly; SHE WAS ONLY A BIRD IN A GILDED CAGE

She's only a bird in a gilded cage,
A beautiful sight to see
You may think she's happy and free from care
She's not, though she seems to be.

Kathy seems to be listening for a moment

KATHY: I know you have been so good to me Ambrose. But sometimes a girl just wants – you know – to dance. And dance...and dance...
BERT: You want to dance, gel? We can do that here. You are looking at the dance king of Mayfair....

He clears a space, and puts on a record – DANCE ON by the SHADOWS.

BERT: (bows) Would the lady care to dance?

Lights change to a spotlight on Kathy. She sings along while she and Bert dance together.

Don't talk of love right now, dance on
Although the lights are low, forget it
Wait until we're alone, wait until we go home
Come on please, I don't tease
Just dance on

Don't try and kiss me now, dance on
You might be feeling quite romantic
But we'll dance cheek to cheek
Or we'll miss every beat
Just dance on

Give me the sweet talk when we're leaving
From midnight on it's worth believing

You know the night has just begun
And while the music keeps on playing
Hold me close, hold me near
And I promise you'll hear
How the beat of my heart will dance on

Give me the sweet talk when we're leaving …

Ambrose cuts the song short

BERT: Bruce Forsyth, that son of a bitch! How could you. After all I've done for you.

KATHY: I...I don't know what you mean…

BERT: You think I don't know. I know everything about you, gel. Everything you do, everywhere you go...don't forget that. You've been seeing him behind my back

KATHY: Have you been following me?
BERT: Can you blame me?
KATHY: It wasn't like that Ambrose. I was just lonely. You're never around when I'm on tour.
BERT: And that makes it okay?
KATHY: I didn't say that.
BERT: Forsyth is married.
KATHY: You're married, Ambrose .
BERT: ! My wife lives in America. I haven't seen her in twenty years. Not that I fucking want to.
KATHY: You're **still** married.
BERT: Never mind my wife. We all make mistakes. And that was a mistake. She was a mistake. My life is here. In England. With the band. With you. Why am I talking about my wife anyway? (pause) Look, I made you, I can fucking break you.
KATHY: I'm so confused Ambrose. I know what I did was wrong......
BERT: (interrupting) Are you going to leave me?
KATHY: I love you Ambrose. I would never leave you. (pause) You stopped making love to me. I thought you didn't love me anymore.
BERT: That's just...it's a physical thing. The doctor's prescribing me some...stuff. Soon be as right as rain again. (he holds her, a tender moment) Of course I love you. Are you sure you're not going to leave me?
KATHY: Oh darling, yes, I'm sure.
BERT: Good, You are not working with Forsyth again though.
KATHY: I thought we were doing a summer season together at the Opera House in Blackpool?
BERT: Not a chance. We don't need him. He can't dance, and he can't sing. In twenty years time they will still be talking about Kathy Kirby - while...Jack The Lad Forsyth will be working in pantomime - if he's lucky.
KATHY: But he's such a big star...
BERT: You're a big star - and don't you forget it, gel. That's why he's been hanging onto your coat-tails. And anyway, the Winter Gardens have offered you a summer season on your own

The Kathy Kirby Show, how does that sound?
KATHY: It sounds wonderful. I just hope I can do it justice.
BERT: Of course you will. (pause) Is something the matter?
KATHY: No, it's nothing. I'm just feeling a bit under the weather. (smiles) I am sure you know best, Ambrose.
BERT: You bet I do. And don't you forget it.

Kathy looks much happier now; she begins to apply her make-up etc. Bert watches her for a moment.

BERT: Did I ever tell you what my ideal woman would look like? A cross between Marilyn Monroe and Diana Dors.
KATHY: (who is painting her lips a glossy red) Like this?
BERT: Yes. How did you guess?
KATHY: You talk in your sleep. (she laughs) And you do have a lot of pictures of Marilyn. Did you ever meet her?
BERT: Oh sure. Several times. She sang a few numbers with the band one night.
We hear the sound of the BERT AMBROSE BAND playing in the background. Bert directs briefly before it fades.
KATHY: Oh really. What songs? Please, I want to know, Ambrose. Marilyn singing with the Bert Ambrose Band. Imagine!
BERT: I can't remember. It was a long time ago

KATHY: She sang 'Diamonds Are A girl's Best Friend'. You told me so, Ambrose. Don't you remember?
Bert ignores her; she sings a verse of it
KATHY: A kiss on the hand may be quite continental
But diamonds are a girl's best friend
A kiss may be grand... but it won't pay the rental
on your humble flat
Or help you at the automat
Men grow cold as girls grow old
And we all lose our charms in the end
But square cut or pear shape these rocks don't
lose their shape
Diamonds are a girl's best friend

Kathy's singing gradually trails off

BERT: You could be the English Marilyn.
KATHY: Is that who you want me to be...baby?
BERT: It would be a good career move.
KATHY: A good career move? Is that all it means to you?
BERT: Of course not. It's just that you remind me so much of her. I don't think you realise how beautiful you are, Kathy
KATHY: I already feel like her. You've got me dressing and looking like her. Can't I just be plain old Kathy Kirby?
BERT: You will never be plain, Kathy.
KATHY: And I want to sing pop songs. Like Dusty, Sandy...Cilla...
BERT: You're not a pop singer, darling…
KATHY: But I am. I really am. I could have sung that...that song better than Cilla…(long pause) If I had been given the chance.
BERT: Come on! You're bigger and better than that. Big voice, big band sound. You're a torch singer, someone who sings about love and loss, and the pain of experience. The power of torch-singing lies in its effect on the listener – and you have that power. Anybody can sing a pop song, but you...you can sing anything. Now, show me what you can do.

She sings ANYONE WHO HAD A HEART

KATHY: Anyone who ever loved, could look at me
And know that I love you
Anyone who ever dreamed, could look at me
And know I dream of you
Knowing I love you so
Anyone who had a heart
Would take me in his arms and love me, too
You couldn't really have a heart and hurt me,
Like you hurt me and be so untrue
What am I to do

Every time you go away, I always say
This time it's goodbye, dear
Loving you the way I do
I take you back, without you I'd die dear
Knowing I love you so
Anyone who had a heart
Would take me in his arms and love me, too
You couldn't really have a heart and hurt me,
Like you hurt me and be so untrue
What am I to do

Knowing I love you so
Anyone who had a heart
Would take me in his arms and love me, too
You couldn't really have a heart and hurt me,
Like you hurt me and be so untrue
Anyone who had a heart would love me too
Anyone who had a heart would surely
Take me in his arms and always love me
Why won't you

*****

New scene. Kathy in her 1980's dressing room

KATHY: I'm not doing any interviews, MJ
MJ: Too late. All they want to do is ask you a few questions and take a few photos. It will be good publicity, get you some bookings.
Several reporters rush in as MJ speaks
REP1: Do you have a child by Tom Jones Miss Kirby?
KATHY: What! (flustered) No, I bloody don't!
REP2: Rumour has it you stabbed Dusty Springfield - is it true?
KATHY: I don't believe this! (shouts) No it's bloody not true.

REP1: Did Bert Ambrose spend five million pounds of your money?

KATHY: Yes, he bloody did. (*she becomes aggressive and hysterical*) I have enough of this. Get out! (She throws several objects at the reporters) Go on, get out!

MJ hurriedly ushers them out. They stand outside the door as MJ tries to placate her.

KATHY: Is that part of the good publicity? Did I stab.....!

She picks up an ashtray and is about to throw it when MJ takes it from her.

KATHY: Did you read that story last week? THE STARLET WHO FADED AWAY.

MJ: I gave it a quick glance.

KATHY: I was never a bloody starlet, MJ

MJ: Of course you weren't. You were a star. The biggest. Everybody knows that.

KATHY: I am not talking to anybody. I don't have to. I'm calling my lawyer. You tell those bloody reporters they are not printing a word. That Polly Toynbee was the same a few weeks ago. Pretending to be interested in me. Pretending to care. Then slipping in all those awful questions. Was Ambrose a father-figure substitute? Stuff like that.. And then she wanted to know about my father. Okay, so father deserted us when I was about seven...but that happened to lots of families. And we did okay without him. Look at me! And my sister Pat didn't do too badly either. We never missed him not being there. Alright, he was a lousy bastard, but that doesn't mean I want the whole world to know it.

MJ: I thought the story was very favourable to you.

KATHY; She tricked me. They all tricked me. Just like this lot are trying to do.

MJ: Look, calm down, will you? They're only trying to help. You invited them here, remember?

KATHY: I don't care. They're fired. You're all fired. I don't want your bookings. Take them all away *(she sees a cameraman and shouts*) And you can turn that ... effing camera off. Go on, get out the lot of you.

MJ ushers them all away, talking to them as he does so. Kathy sits in her chair and broods.

MJ: What brought that on? Five minutes ago you were the picture of happiness. Now, It's like you are two different persons. (pause) Where is the real Kathy Kirby?

KATHY: I don't know where she is. Ambrose is the only one who knows.

Kathy has been pulling at her hair during this. She pulls out some and looks at it.

MJ: What's the matter with your hair?

KATHY: It's mummy. She's been pulling out my hair again.

MJ: Why would she do that?

KATHY: Because she wants to punish me. I know her secret, you see. And she doesn't like it. Look! *(she shows him the 'bald' patch)*

MJ: What secret?

KATHY: She drinks. A lot.

MJ: Runs in the family, does it?

KATHY: I'm not a bloody alcoholic, if that's what you're implying.

She tries on a turban to hide the hair patch. She also puts on a pair of dark glasses

KATHY: Don't you think I look like Norma?

MJ: Norma?

KATHY: Norma Desmond. Come on, MJ! Sunset Boulevard.

MJ: Yeah. Maybe.

KATHY: Well, I feel like her. Sometimes I wish I could just hide myself away, and....*(she discards the turban)*...just be...normal.

MJ: I think maybe ...you need to see a psychiatrist.

KATHY: That's what Ambrose thinks too. But I will prove him wrong. (shouts) Do you hear that, Ambrose?

MJ: *(shakes his head*) Maybe I'm the one who should see the psychiatrist. *(pause)* I have lots of work in the book for you and now you say you are not doing it anymore.

KATHY: How can I work at present when I don't have my own voice or body?

MJ: That's stupid.

KATHY: That's the way I feel

MJ: I don't think you realise what you are saying. (*pause)* I haven't told you this but your name is mud everywhere I go these days.

KATHY: That's not true. People still love me. How many standing ovations did I get the other night at...at..wherever it was

MJ: That's the punters, darling. And most of them were full of cheap lager and gin-and-tonics. They'd clap at their own reflections. I'm talking about promoters. Nobody is willing to take a chance with you anymore. It's as if there's a self destruct button inside you, and when things are going well you have to press it - again and again. You're destroying your career.

KATHY: What Career? That died with Ambrose. I'm a perfectionist, and if things are not right – the music, the arrangements, whatever – then I speak my mind. If that's being difficult...well...

MJ: You argue with everybody. (pause) I I don't think I can do this anymore, Kathy.

KATHY: Close the door on your way out MJ. If you don't want to look after my affair there are plenty out there who will.

New scene

'THIS IS YOUR LIFE' TV show 1983. Stuart Henry (Deejay)is the guest of honour. Kathy is appearing as a guest. She is dozing in her dressing room. In her mind she is performing. She sings a few lines from I CAN GIVE YOU ANYTHING BUT LOVE.

KATHY: I can't give you anything but love...baby

That's the only thing there's plenty of...baby

Dream a while...scheme a while

You're sure to find....happiness and I guess

All those things you've pined for

Kathy wakes up, disorientated, confused.

KATHY: MJ...MJ... what's going on?

MJ appears.

MJ: What's up?

KATHY: Where's Bert. (*she looks around and doesn't see anybody*) have the dancers gone?

MJ: (*picking up her bottle of tablets*) Oh Christ. Do you know where you are?

KATHY: Blackpool?

MJ: No! You are appearing on This is Your Life. (*holds his head*) Jesus.

KATHY: Who gave them permission? I'm not bloody doing it.

MJ: Not your life...thank God. It's Stuart Henry's. You know, the DeeJay.

KATHY: I always think deejays are like eunuchs. They know how to do it but they can't do it themselves.

MJ: Do what?

KATHY: Sing. Perform

MJ: I think you mean theatre critics.

KATHY: Deejays too. They think they are a law unto themselves most of them. Bert says you have to bribe them all to get them to play your records on the radio. Stuart Henry...I don't think I ever even met him. What am I doing here?

MJ: You're doing a slow, sexy number, darling. Surely you remember?

KATHY: I do now. I need a drink then before I face that lot.

MJ: Yeah you do. Lots of it. Black coffee. Don't go away. *(he rushes out)*

KATHY: *(picking up Benjy)* We can do better than that Benjy, can't we.

She helps herself to a pill, and washes it down with a drink from a bottle retrieved from her handbag. Presently she reverts to her previous state. Bert comes into view.

BERT: Were you makin' whoopee with Forsyth again? Come on, you had better come clean.

KATHY: (*in her mind she is young Kathy*). Tell him. Tell him the truth. That he's no good. That he can't satisfy you anymore. ((She shouts) YOU CAN'T SATISFY ME ANY MORE! How long are you going to keep this up Ambrose? We can't go to a restaurant or out for a drink without you flying off the handle lately.

BERT: As long as it takes. You deceived me all those months Kathy. You might still be doing so. It's got me so worked up I can't think straight anymore.

KATHY: Is that why you are turning down work for me? Decent work, I mean.

BERT: That's not true. I have you working all the time.

KATHY: Yeah. What about that Hollywood Producer?. A three picture deal he said. He wants me. Or he did. Imagine what that could do for my career.

BERT: (lamely) I'm still working on it

KATHY: Liar! (pause) My affair with Bruce finished a long time ago. I told you that. Why don't you believe me?

BERT: If only I could. You're a beautiful woman, Kathy. Any man would want you. I wanted you the first night I set eyes on you. There's someone else now, isn't there? There must be.

Kathy sees her younger self again

KATHY: Tell him about the others. Go on, tell him. I insist. *(no response*) Okay then, I'll tell him myself. I had an affair with Tom Jones. Do you hear me Ambrose? A red hot affair right under your nose. And Jimmy Saville. He was all over me like a rash. Do you recall telling me to go and get some experience before you would take me into your bed?

BERT: I didn't mean bloody Saville.

KATHY: I took your advice. It was easy. Remember that time he was manager of the Ilford Palais? I just locked him in my dressing room one night. And we did it.

BERT: Saville just likes little girls. The younger the better.

He doesn't see the irony of his statement. Kathy snorts in derision.

KATHY: You can talk!

BERT: You must have heard the rumours. His Rolls Royce, after Top of The Pops is over, filled with teenage girls. Twelve, fourteen year olds, so they tell me. What goes on in Saville's Rolls?...that's what the bloody hacks should be after, not puerile stories about the likes of me and you. (laughs) To be honest, I always thought he was a bit of Nancy-boy.

KATHY: He might have been a lot of things, but that wasn't one of them. Just so as you know - He was a real man. Do you hear me? A real man.

There is no immediate response but it is clear that Bert is hurt

BERT: I hope he treated you in the style I accustomed you to.

KATHY: Accustomed! You! You spent all my money, you bastard. And you lied to me all the time

BERT: Only little ones, my dear. White ones.

KATHY: Black...black! How much was I earning a week, Ambrose, at my peak?

BERT: *(barks out)* Ten thousand.

KATHY: Forty Thousand you lying bastard. How much were you giving me?

BERT: *(barks out)* Three thousand.

KATHY: One thousand you stingy bastard.

BERT: There were lots of incidentals...

KATHY: Yeah. Crockfords, The Clermont, The Cromwellian Club, to name a few. You were enjoying yourself without me - but not without my money, of course! I remember arriving at a Casino in Mayfair once, having tracked you down there. The management invited me in with the words "come in Miss Kirby, you might as well have a look around. This place was built with all your money Ambrose lost at our other casinos". I thought it was a joke at the time. Well, what's good for the goose is good for the gander.

MJ rushes in and brings Kathy back to reality

MJ: Come on Kathy, your cue. Don't forget, Stuart Henry.

Kathy gathers herself and walks into the TV studio

****

<u>**New scene**</u>.

Kathy is performing on the Les Dawson show on TV. She is waiting to go onstage and is in a side-room discussing forthcoming plans with Bert. It is 1971. She screams when she sees a vase of plastic flowers on the side table

KATHY: Oh my God! Those are those plastic!.

BERT: Give me strength, somebody! (*he picks up some of the flowers and throws them away*) Doesn't anybody know it's bad luck to have plastic flowers anywhere near a studio? Bloody clueless!

Kathy, I think we have a chance with that new ITV show, what's it called., Wheeltappers and..? *(he makes a face and rubs his chest).*

KATHY: Are you okay, Ambrose?

BERT: It's just indigestion. Oooh... *(he almost collapses)* Could I have some water...no, some brandy?

KATHY: Help! Can I have some help here?

Ambrose moans

KATHY: Ambrose! Are you in pain?

BERT: Of course I'm in pain. Where's the damn brandy. (*his speech is a bit slurred)*

KATHY: I don't think that would be a good idea. Where does it hurt?

BERT: *(slurred)* Here *(chest)* Here *(left arm)* Here *(jaw)*

KATHY: We need an ambulance. I think you might be having a heart attack. Oh Ambrose. *(she goes and comforts him*) Wake up! Don't leave me Ambrose. *(he doesn't respond*) Help! Someone help him.

We hear a voice over the intercom 'You are on in two minutes Miss Kirby'.

KATHY: I can't go on. Not with this happening.

BERT: (*reviving momentarily*) Go into the studio and sing your song, Kathy. Do as I say, I'm your manager, I know best. Go on, I'll be alright.

You have to. Your audience is out there waiting. There's twelve million live TV viewers waiting to see you.

KATHY: But Ambrose...what if you need me?

Bert groans again, clearly in pain

BERT: Go! There's nothing you can do for me right now. I'll soon be in the best of hands, receiving the best of care.

KATHY: Well, yes...I suppose...

BERT: Do it for me, Kathy

Kathy sings SECRET LOVE

KATHY: Now I shout it from the highest hills
Even told the golden daffodils
Once I had a secret love
That lived within the heart of me
All too soon my secret love
Became impatient to be free

So I told a friendly star
The way that dreamers often do
Just how wonderful you are
And why I am so in love with you

Now I shout it from the highest hills
Even told the golden daffodils

At last my heart's an open door
And my secret love's no secret anymore.

End of Act one.

ACT 2

Late 1970's Kathy has been evicted from her home and is now confined to a mental Hospital. LARAINE McKAY arrives, carrying a big bunch of flowers, and a bag. She has cropped dark hair and dresses like a man.

LAR: Hello Kathy. I'm Larraine. Laraine McKay. I did write to say I was coming.

KATHY: Yes. I got your letter. You are most kind

LAR: I am such a big fan of yours. *(she hold out the flowers)* These are for you.

KATHY: Thank you so much. (*she takes the flowers*) The...nurses will find something to put them in.

LAR: How could they put you in here? A mental hospital!

KATHY: It was either here or prison I guess. I had nowhere else to go.

LAR: Why would they put you in prison? You did nothing wrong.

KATHY I was declared bankrupt. Then I was evicted from my home, and charged with not paying my bill when I stayed at the Mount Royal Hotel. The court decided I was homeless and ordered me to stay here awaiting the trial. I think the judge thinks it's a hostel for the homeless.

LAR: you poor thing…

KATHY Who cares? My life ended when Ambrose died My public life, anyway. Who can I turn to now? I have no manager, no mentor, everything's just gone to pieces.

LAR: I'm here for you. Whatever I can do.

KATHY: I don't know what to say. Why would you do all this for me?

LAR: Because I like you. And us...girls of the world have to stick together.

KATHY: Girls of the world? I suppose we are. (pause) You look like a...I don't know... a bit…

LAR: Lesbian?

KATHY: No! You're not, are you? (pause) You are?

LAR: Does it shock you?

KATHY: Well I...no, course not

LAR: Some of your best friends are lesbians, eh!

KATHY: Well...one or two are.

LAR: Like Dusty?

KATHY: Dusty is not exactly a friend. (laughs) In fact someone once put out a story that I tried to stab her.

LAR: She tried a move on you!

KATHY: No. It wasn't true. (laughs again) I swear, it wasn't

LAR: That's better. You're smiling again.

KATHY: Yes, I am. Come and sit near me Laraine.

Larraine comes and sits close

KATHY: The real reason they sent me here is that I took an overdose of sleeping pills And I started hearing voices in my head.

LAR: So you are really a…

KATHY: Head case? Do I look bonkers?

LAR: No. But I probably do.

KATHY: They think I might be a bit...schizophrenic

LAR: Wow! But you're getting treatment, right?

KATHY: Medication. My smarties, I call them. Different colours.

LAR: What about your family? Can't they help? Your sister Pat?

KATHY: You know about...Pat?

LAR: know all about you. I have followed your career since I was this high. *(she indicates)*

KATHY: My stalker!

LAR: No! I wouldn't do anything to harm you. I just love your voice, your personality...I'm your biggest fan

KATHY: (pats her hand) I'm only kidding, Laraine - my nice, kind stalker. I haven't seen or spoken to Pat for ...must be ten years. Ambrose didn't want my family too close – interfering too much, he said.

LAR: Your brother, Douglas.?

KATHY: He has his own life. They all have

LAR: And your mother?

KATHY: She never liked Ambrose. She always suspected he was spending my money. She tried to shove him out the window of the flat once. We were three stories up. I had to drag her away.
(pause)
We have never got on. She smothers me, she always has. I couldn't stay with her. We'd only end up killing each other after a few days.

LAR: I saw it all happening on that television programme. You being evicted from your home. The bailiffs dragging you out and taking all your lovely stuff away. Why was it all on TV?

KATHY: I phoned up and told the TV company about it. They sent a crew around. I must have been crazy, but I thought it might stop the bailiffs from, you know...But they still threw me out.

LAR: Poor Kathy!

KATHY: I owed money to the tax man, everyone. I couldn't find my money. They said it had all gone. That Ambrose had gambled it all away. I knew he liked to play the tables – he said it helped him unwind – but how could anyone lose millions?

LAR: I cried for you Kathy. No, I cried with you. *(she holds Kathy's hand)*

KATHY: I am so alone.

LAR: No, you are not! I will write to you every day if I can't visit you. *(she hands Kathy a bag of coins)*

KATHY: What's this?

LAR: It's coins. For the phone. So you can ring me whenever you want.

KATHY: (emotional over the bag of coins) I don't know what to say.

LAR: Us girls have to stick together. Right?

KATHY: Right. If I had somewhere to stay I think I might be allowed to leave this place.

LAR: You can come and stay with me. Share my room, if you like.

****

New scene

Kathy has been released into Laraine's care and they are having a weekend break in Brighton.

LAR: I just love Brighton, don't you?

KATHY: Bert always liked it. We came here a lot. I said it suited him to a tee. Full of spivs, just like himself. I love the Hippodrome, love performing there.

LAR: Ambrose a spiv! He was the picture of sophistication.

KATHY: That was just an image. He was most at home in the smoky gambling dens of Mayfair and Soho. And among the touts and spivs at the Brighton races.

LAR: Spending your money!

KATHY: Always my money. He even stole my jewellery and pawned it. I should have listened to Eva Petulengro.

LAR: Who?

KATHY: She was a Romany fortune teller I went to see when we were here in 1970. She told me that he would be dead within a year, and to leave him, or I would regret it for the rest of my life.

LAR: She was right?

KATHY: She **was** right, and I **have** regretted it ever since. Bert just laughed when I told him. Said she was a fake. I think I am finished with men, Larraine.

LAR: But they love you so much! Their Blonde Bombshell!

KATHY: The trouble is they love me so much they wind up taking all my money. I think this weekend in Brighton is just what I needed, Laraine. At first I was so confused, but you have shown me such kindness, listened to my problems, and got me out of that horrible mental institute. I feel so safe with you.

LAR: I'll always look after you.

LAR: Sex is a great healer, Kathy. And when it's with someone you love, that's even better. That's why I think we should get married. So what do you say my lovely blonde bombshell?

KATHY: You're serious?

LAR: Of course I am.

KATHY: I don't see how we can. I mean, it's not legal, is it?

LAR: It wouldn't be a real marriage of course, not in the eyes of the law anyway. It would be just a bonding ceremony. But it would be real enough for me, Kathy Kirby

KATHY: Kathleen O'Rourke, actually. That's my real name. You know, this is all so...so surreal. I am going to wake up in a minute.

LAR: Let me pinch you then. *(she does so)*

Kathy squeals.

LAR: See, it's real. What do you say? Will you marry me Kathy Kirby stroke O'Rourke?

KATHY: (laughing) Seeing as you put it like that, how could I refuse!

They dance wildly around the stage in celebration.

****

New scene

KATHY: I had an abortion in 1964.

LAR: You don't say! Not that I'm surprised with your looks. Let me guess...Tom Jones.

KATHY: No such luck!

BERT: Bruce Forsyth?

KATHY: It was Bert.

LAR: Did you tell him?

KATHY: What would have been the point? He was already married, remember?

LAR: Nothing that a quickie five dollar divorce in Reno couldn't fix.

KATHY: I know what his reply would have been. 'It wouldn't look good to your fans, Kathy'. So I had an abortion. I told nobody.

LAR: Not even your mother?

KATHY: Especially not my mother. You're the first person I've ever told.

LAR: I don't think I would be brave enough to go through something like that on my own.

KATHY: It wasn't the only baby I lost. (long pause) I did get married…

LAR: I do know. His name was Fred Pye, wasn't it?

KATHY: Yes. A few years ago. It was the most nervous moment of my life. I was petrified. It was worse than my opening night as a singer. But by now I was sick of touring, sick of making comebacks, so I decided to settle down and be a housewife. I even managed to get pregnant. Then one day when I was playing with our Yorkshire terrier, I fell and had a miscarriage...

Fred Pye appears. There is blood on his arm and on his face.

FRED: You stabbed me you mad bitch!

KATHY: I wanted that child more than anything in the world.

FRED: So you stick a knife in my arm?

KATHY: You should have been more attentive to me. Ambrose wouldn't have let it happen.

FRED: You're fucking mad, woman. You need locking up.

KATHY: I am so heartbroken. I don't think I'll ever recover. (*pause*)

FRED: I should call the police

KATHY: The neighbours have probably already called the press.

FRED: Sod the neighbours.

KATHY: We'll need a cover story. Let's tell them you walked into one of those exposed beams in the lounge.

FRED: And what about this three inch gash in my arm. And all those broken windows? You're losing touch with reality, Kathy.

KATHY: I'm sorry. I'm so sorry. I didn't mean to...

FRED: So am I. But we can't go on like this. I am ending this marriage.

Fred exits

MJ appears

MJ: Where's Laraine?

KATHY: I don't know. I haven't seen her for a few days. I'm worried....

MJ: I'll tell you where she is. She's locked up. In jail

KATHY: I don't understand...

MJ: She was caught stealing cheques. And they locked her up. They weren't yours, were they?

KATHY: O f course not. How...how did you find out?

MJ opens the door

MJ: This is how.

Lots of noise; reporters clamouring, shouting etc. A TV reporter is commenting.

VOICES: Where is Laraine McKay? Is the marriage still going ahead?

TV: Here comes Cathy Kirby now. Miss Kirby, is it true that Laraine McKay has been arrested?

MJ closes the door again. Kathy looks very flustered.

MJ: Well?

KATHY: Well what? I don't know what's going on. (pause) They know everything...the reporters?

MJ: It would appear so. Marriage? Bloody marriage!

KATHY: It wasn't real....

MJ: Of course it wasn't. Are you crazy, Kathy? Jesus! Can't you see she was playing you?

KATHY: No. That's not true. We...we had....(pause) Where is she now?

MJ: I am told she is in Holloway Prison. She was only out on bail these last few months. That's how she was able to meet you. Then her mother and brother refused to continue to stand bail when they found out about...you, so she has been locked up again.

TV: Oh God! What am I going to do?

****

New scene.

Bert reappears

BERT: She was only after your money.

KATHY: That's a laugh coming from you. Most of the money she took she spent on me. She was given three years in gaol. (laughs) She got three years for a few thousand, you got nothing for millions. I visited her a few times, but I knew that it wasn't going to work out in the long run so I ended the relationship.

BERT: Money, the root of all evil! I hear Anita Harris lost a million pounds to a fraudulent Swiss bank.

KATHY: Dear Anita, only a million! You gambled away over five million of mine.

BERT: Five million! As much as that?

KATHY: Don't you have any conscience?

BERT: It was only money, Kathy.

KATHY: Only my money.

Bert studies her and shakes his head

BERT: Oh Kathy, Kathy, look at you now. You lived a very glamorous life. You had lots of furs, diamonds, ate in the best restaurants, and your clothes were hand-made.

KATHY: I dressed and behaved in whatever way you wanted me to look.

BERT: You wanted for nothing.

KATHY: I was your invention. And when you were no longer there your invention couldn't survive on her own. You were the best and worst thing that ever happened to me.

BERT: I made you a star,

KATHY: But you exploited me. You never returned the love I had for you. You were a cold, cold man, interested only in money. You only ever saw me as a cash-cow.

BERT: That's not true, baby.

KATHY: I needed men in my life, I know that now. I needed you in my life (she cries) I need you in my life.

BERT: Like all stars, you are fragile, you need careful handling. All the stars I've known are egomaniacs, suffer delusions, and begin to believe their own publicity. You are no different. Remember how you would come home from a show and sit in a chair until seven or eight in the morning, and talk the biggest load of rubbish I'd ever heard? It would take you a couple of days to get back into your stride again. I was worried about your mental health, Kathy. I tried to get you to see a psychiatrist but you wouldn't have it.

KATHY: You thought I was a schizophrenic.

BERT: You were. You are.

KATHY: Did you want me certified?

BERT: Of course not. I want you to get help.

KATHY: That would make it easier to get your hands on my money.

BERT: I love you, baby. That's the only reason. It's not easy for me either, you know. The generation gap is driving me crazy. I know I will lose you in the end. And there's this jealousy raging inside me that's driving me crazy. Making me... ah, I'm just an old fool. (pause) Look, I just want you to get help before it is too late.

KATHY: Whatever I am Ambrose, you made me that way.

Kathy begins shouting

KATHY: Oh God, I hate this goldfish existence. It was you - you caused all this. If you hadn't died… WHY DID YOU DIE?

She sings ANYONE WHO HAD A HEART, (c) Hal David - Burt Bacharach, the one song she always felt she was born to sing

KATHY:

Anyone who ever loved could look at me
And know that I love you
Anyone who ever dreamed could look at me
And know I dream of you, knowing I love you so

Anyone who had a heart
Would take me in his arms and love me too
You couldn't be another heart that hurt me
Like you hurt me and be so untrue, what am I to do

Every time you go away, I always say
This time it's goodbye, dear
Loving you the way I do
I take you back, without you I'd die, dear, knowing I love you so

Anyone who had a heart
Would take me in his arms and love me too

You couldn't be another heart that hurt me
Like you hurt me and be so untrue, what am I to do

End of scene

****

ACT 3

Years later. Kathy is at home, seated in her armchair, wearing a turban. She can be wearing dark glasses if desired.
She dances a little, watching herself in her full-length mirror as she sings.
Her niece SARAH come on stage. Sarah looks just like a younger Kathy. She looks at some framed pictures of Kathy performing.

SARAH: Where was this taken, Aunt Kathy?

KATHY: Let me look. That's easy. The mid 1980's. It was the last time I tried to kick start my career. A bingo hall in Chatham. I performed a thirty minute spot between sessions. 600 bingo players paid 30p each to see me.

SARAH: A bingo hall. Really, Aunt Kathy!

SARAH: Really. It may not sound like much, but I was overjoyed the way the audience treated me. They clapped and cheered me for ten minutes. I must admit I cried. They were really wonderful. But I knew it was over. The magic had gone for me. If you lose the magic it shows in your face, and I could see it had gone from mine. I knew then that I couldn't do it anymore. You never saw me perform in my heyday, did you, Sarah-Jane

SARAH: No. I would have liked to of course. Mum often talked about how you and her sometimes performed together.

KATHY: Pat was a fair singer in her own right. She even recorded a couple of songs.

SARAH: You were the real star though.

KATHY: It hasn't done me much good, has it, the way things have worked out? But you're not here to reminisce about my good old days, are you?

SARAH: No. You must give me power of attorney over your affairs, Aunt Kathy. Otherwise your money – what you have left of it – will eventually disappear. (she looks at a document in her hand) This cheque for instance, for fifty pounds, to somebody called Tony...

KATHY: Oh Sarah-Jane, that is Taxi Tony. He's lovely. He takes me anywhere I want to go. He also does some shopping for me...

SARAH: Hmmm. And this one, for one hundred pounds? What's that for?

KATHY: Let me see? (she looks) Oh yes. I had no cash in the house so I asked Mark to cash a cheque for me.... Mark visits me nearly every week...

SARAH: Mark, Tony...who are these people?

KATHY: They are my friends. My only friends these days. Everyone in show-business has forgotten me.

SARAH I doubt that. It's not good enough, Aunt Kathy. They are taking advantage of you. You are being exploited. The money coming in from all those new CD's and the other re-releases – it's going out faster than it's coming in as far as I can see.

KATHY: It's only money, Sarah Jane. And don't forget I lived with the master at spending my money. (laughs) Millions of pounds of it. (pause)

SARAH: That's why choosing the right man is so important.

KATHY: You don't choose who you fall in love with. Did you marry for love, Sarah?

SARAH: Well yes, I suppose I did.

KATHY: Yet here you are, divorced.

SARAH: I never pretended I was perfect.

KATHY: Are you going to marry Mark?

SARAH: What?

KATHY: Mark Thatcher. You are seeing him again?

SARAH: It's no big secret. And we are both single again.

KATHY: So?

SARAH: We are waiting for his divorce to become final. Then we'll see.

KATHY: Lady Sarah-Jane. That has a nice ring to it.

SARAH: Don't be silly Aunt Kathy!

KATHY: It's true. He's inherited his father's title so you become 'Lady'. And with a former Prime Minister for a mother-in-law. You must bring him along here for tea sometime and let me have a look at him. Don't forget I'm an expert in unsuitable men.

SARAH; Mark is very busy these days.

KATHY: I am not at all sure he is right for you. He's a...well, he's a bit of a crook, isn't he!

SARAH: Of course he's not. All that trouble in Africa was a misunderstanding.

KATHY: But he was fined – and given a suspended sentence. Wasn't he a mercenary or gun-runner or something?

SARAH: It was nothing like that...it was all very complicated. Anyway, we are not here to talk about Mark or me. This about you, sorting your life out, making things easier for you. From what I can see these so-called friends have been taking you for a ride. (she looks at some more papers) All this wine and spirits, who has been drinking that?

KATHY: I like a glass of something in the evening. With my friends.

Bert and MJ now appear. It should be clear that Kathy's illness - her schizophrenia - hasn't disappeared. It is under control to a certain extent, but does flare up occasionally

BERT: And with me.

KATHY: Be quiet, Bert. I'm not talking to you.

BERT: Why? Because I told you off earlier for ringing the police and telling them someone was trying to steal your voice.

KATHY: But they were!

BERT: And what did they say, the police?

KATHY: They threatened to charge me with wasting police time..

SARAH: Your medical condition specifically forbids all alcohol. You are killing yourself. And your friends are helping you. I am sorry, Aunt Kathy, but you must let me put your affairs in order. You must sign this document giving me power of attorney. Otherwise a court will order you taken into care…

KATHY: Where were you when I needed you? Where was everybody else in my family?

SARAH: You made your feelings clear to them. Many times. Nobody realised your situation was so bad. So chaotic. (pause) I have been delegated to sort out your affairs, and I intend to do it properly.

KATHY: I don't want to go into care. I want to stay here, in my own home. Will you promise that I can stay here?

SARAH: Of course you can.

Kathy takes the document and signs it.

KATHY: I hope I am doing the right thing.

SARAH: You are.

Sarah takes the paperwork and fades from view

KATHY: I really hope I did the right thing. It's been several weeks since I saw any of my friends. I am sure they will come and see me soon. I **know** they will come and see me soon.

BERT: They won't. You know they won't. Sarah has warned them all off. She's in the driving seat now.

MJ appears

MJ: Don't you wonder why Sarah and her mother suddenly turned up after all these years? Why they have taken control. They can smell money

BERT: The aristocracy always could.

KATHY: What money?

BERT: Your dear departed aunt in America. Your legacy is quite substantial, isn't it? Or will be when you get your hands on it. Or someone else does. And then there's this revival in your music, all those re-issued cd's and so on…(laughs) It's a shame I'm not still around, gel

KATHY: No, thank you! What are you doing here MJ?. We parted company years ago.

MJ: Someone has to look out for you. You are surrounded by gangsters and cut-throats. And a family who abandoned you for over thirty years.

KATHY: It was my own fault. I was difficult to live with.

MJ: No, it's not your fault. They all swung off your coat tails during the good times. Spongers the lot of them.

BERT: Nice to know I wasn't the only one.

MJ: And Terry, your own brother-in-law how much did he siphon off for his own use?

BERT: Terry?

KATHY: He became my financial advisor after you...after you…

MJ: And he took you to the cleaners.

BERT: So that's how he got his leg on the ladder...When I knew him he didn't have a pot pourri to piss in. At least I had the talent to go with my…

KATHY: Deviousness? Crookedness?

She takes a bottle of wine from a cupboard and pours herself a generous glass. She takes a tablet from a bottle and drinks it with her wine. The others have 'vanished' by now.

KATHY; I have my good days and my bad days, but I get by. Yes, I get by. Some people say I still try to behave and live my life like the star was all those years ago. That I'm living in the past. Well maybe I , but....(she shrugs)...life on stage was always easier for me than it ever was off. For the past 20 years I have hidden myself away in this flat, surviving on my memories, welfare benefits and the occasional gifts from fans.

She looks around her

KATHY: I once had a home worth half a million, investments, diamonds, minks, and property, but now this is my home. (she looks around) As you can see, it's a dump. There's a gloomy winding stairwell, giving the place an eerie, derelict feel. And there's a bare light bulb in the hallway, which makes it look even worse. But I like it that way.(laughs) I am a recluse, like Garbo. And like Garbo I want to be alone. But I am at peace with myself and that in itself is a blessing from God. I feel people within me, so I am not alone. I started to realise how wonderful life can be when you are all alone. All the talking in the world can't make up for thinking.

She sings MAKE SOMEONE HAPPY

KATHY: ***(speaks introduction)***

The sound of applause is delicious,
And it's a thrill to have the world at your feet
The praise of the crowd, well, it's exciting
But I found it's not what makes a life complete
There is one thing you can do for the rest of your days
That's worth more than the applause, the screaming crowds,
the bouquets ...

Make someone happy,
Make just one someone happy.
Make just one heart the heart you sing to.
One smile that cheers you,
One face that lights when it nears you.
One man you're everything to.

Fame, if you win it,
Comes and goes in a minute.
Where is the real stuff in life to cling to?
Love is the answer
Someone to love that's your answer
Once you've found him
Build your world around him
Make someone happy.
Make just, just one someone happy
And you will be happy too.
Fame, if you win it,
Well, it comes and goes in a minute.
Where is the real stuff in life to cling to?
Love is the answer
Someone to love that's your answer
Once you've found him
Build your world around him

Make someone happy.
Make just, just one someone happy
And you will be happy now.

KATHY: My thanks to you and goodnight

CURTAIN. **(c) Tom O'Brien 2018**

47334611R10026

Printed in Poland
by Amazon Fulfillment
Poland Sp. z o.o., Wrocław

Cousin Davey and his beloved trombone

Jim and Moira on their special day.
He was her 'something blue'

Carlos always had an eye for the ladies, an eye for the gents and an eye out for his wife

Doctor Ferguson worked on the animation of plants for years with no success

Charlie and his imaginary demon friend

The bog-snorkelling girls. Marion would go on to snorkel more bogs than anyone else

Lionel, here, patiently waiting for
his turn in the chair

Uncle Bert - he would go on to leave his wife in Arizona. And his wife in London, and the one in Singapore...

With a long, upright handle for ease of use, this dog was a lot of fun

Rex, in his army days. He wasn't blue before he put that belt on

One of Granny's friends. I think she
met him at the bingo

Hamish discovered a kitten in his horn that day

Great Uncle Alexander could tame any chair

Ambrose and Cyril fell in love at first 'sight'

Gerald, our trusted family doctor and exorciser

Auntie Iris never really saw eye to eyes with the family

Stephen, before he ate that photographer

Jerry and his pals on holiday. He was very protective of that rug

Unfortunately we only discovered what Emily was concealing after it was much too late

Terrence and his ghost-bride,
behind, in front and amongst him

Ray, in the bushes again

Ricky and his startle-hound

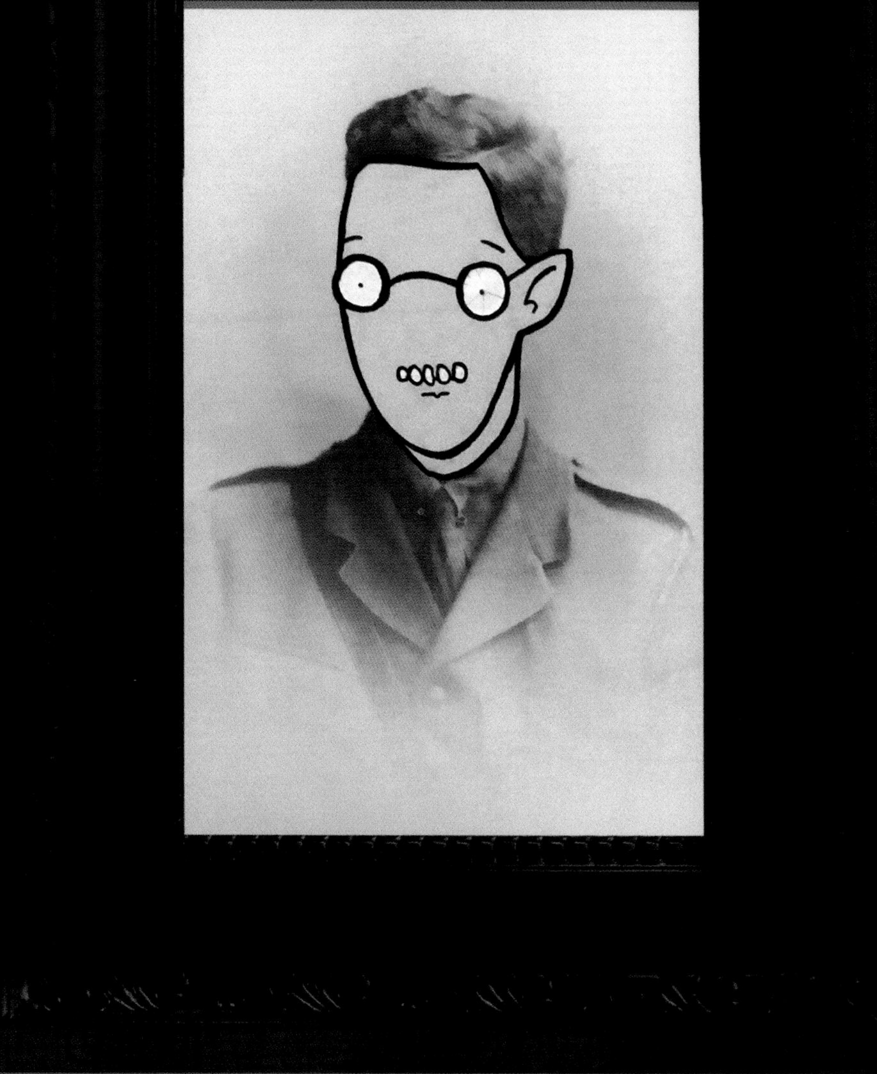

Cedric's sexual magnetism cracked his glasses and crushed the hearts of his lovers

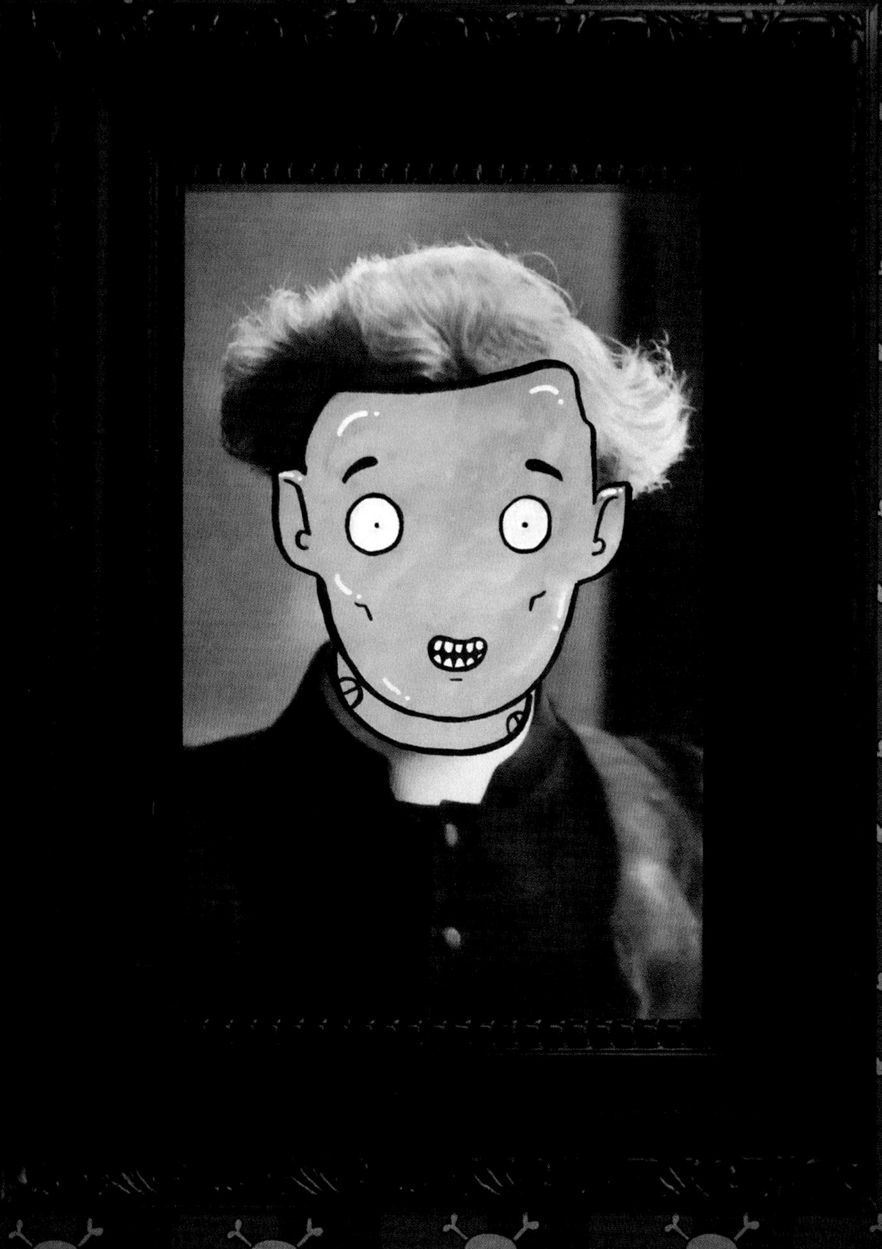

The Reverend Robert Malfunction, after perhaps a little too much communion oil

Noel - White tie, bulging eye.
What a performer!

Max declared that his love for Clara would transcend this mortal realm. Clara replied 'That's nice'

A couple of the youngsters by the sea.
Traditional attire, formal shoes

Suzi made this entire outfit herself, out of a tent

Mr Synester was the friendliest teacher in the school

Great Uncle Ahmed was the most fun, as long as you weren't a person

David loved this hat. He always wore it when he was drunk

The Captain - he did have trouble keeping all his crew on board and sane

The Infamous Tickle Twins. Their double-act was the talk of the town for a short while

Ralph would only let his special friends drink from the fountain

Susanne was underwhelmed with her dog's ability to pull a cart

Margot's major strength was in her fabulous blouses

The gang at the Friday dance. The rule
was armed on the right, armless on the left

Reg and his girls, just before his suit jacket ignited

Outrageous day at the beach! At some points no formal coats were worn

Alfred decided he didn't want to eat people anymore. Now he just eats politicians

Luthor's complexion was darker than a black hole but his hair was a strawberry blonde

Julie fed the firebird everyday until one of them devoured the other

Cousin Andy, in the intermediate stage of his head inflation

Sir Lawrence. His monocle allowed him to see deep into the souls of humans. He didn't see anything of note